How to Compose Music

A Guide to Composing Music for a Musician (or an Eager Beginner) Who Wants to Become a Composer

by Ronald J. Hutchinson

Table of Contents

INTRODUCTION 3

CHAPTER 1 – REVIEWING THE BASICS.............................11

CHAPTER 2 – THE CONCEPTUALIZATION PHASE.........19

CHAPTER 3 – COMPUTER SOFTWARE FOR COMPOSERS 25

CHAPTER 4 – AUDIO PRODUCTION 29

CONCLUSION 33

INTRODUCTION

So you want to be a music composer, eh? Who wouldn't these days? Music is a multi-billion dollar industry, and spans many different genres. However, when we talk about music composition, we usually talk about writing original pieces of music with great form and structure. Modern musicians who write songs are usually called songwriters instead of composers. Composers usually are thought of as people who can score their own music and adhere to the classical form of music. This is not the case, however, as in the true sense of the word, composition is simply making music. Composition is how the composer wants to arrange the various aspects of music - harmony, melody, form, rhythm and timbre - to create his own art. Composition is translating your thoughts and the way you view the world into music. So for anyone who wants to write music, this tutorial is for you.

This tutorial was written for musicians, but if you aren't one, don't despair. You can learn to compose music too even without formal training. For a person to make his or her own music, that person would only have to understand the basics, mentioned above: melody, harmony, rhythm and timbre.

Let's start with melody.

Melody is basically the succession of single notes that are satisfying to the ear. Melody is probably the most important part of the music since it is through the melody that one usually relates to the song. Let's say for example, I play on the piano E-E(flat)-E-E(flat)-E, then what immediately comes to mind (play it on your piano or your guitar and see for yourself)? That's right, it's Fur Elise. When composers past and present come up with a song idea, it will most likely be the melody that enters their head first. With melody in mind, the composer can build upon what he/she has in mind to create a piece of music. In some genres, the beat may come first, but that's probably no more than 5% of music ever made, if even. So now that we understand what melody is, let's now build upon that foundation and define harmony.

Harmony is the combination of two or more musical notes played simultaneously. In simpler terms, harmony is playing other notes simultaneously with the melody. See why melody is so important? When the composer got the melody all or partially figured out, if needed, two or more notes will be added. When two or more notes are sounded together, it is called a chord. This is where we go deeper into music theory, as to understand the different types of chords, we'll have to know things such as keys, major and minor, scales, etc. We'll go further into that later on, but we can brush over them a little here. Remember when we said that melody is a succession of single notes to form something pleasing to the ear? Well, there's one melody that we've all learned from kindergarten or from Sesame Street, and that's "Do-Re-Mi-Fa-So-La-Ti-Do". We call that the musical scale, and more specifically, the major musical scale. From these scales, we derive the keys of the songs. If you don't understand, don't worry. We'll discuss the basics in the following chapter.

Next let's look at rhythm. Rhythm is a pattern of regular beats played throughout the song. In modern popular music, rhythm along with melody, is the most important aspect. In the House genre, for example, the rhythm is usually a steady beat in 4/4 timing that plays steadily and repeatedly. In hip hop, you have a lot of different types of rhythms used, but they usually go over a 2/4 beat. Rhythm is also defined as the pattern in which the melody is sung or played. Culture affects rhythm a lot, and Western popular music borrows a lot of the elements of rhythm from Eastern and other cultures.

Finally there's timbre, which is defined as the character and properties of the music, or how parts of the music sound. Timbre brings in a wide variety of elements including pitch, tone, intensity, etc. To help understand better, we'll use the example of Luciano Pavarotti's version "Nessun Dorma" which he performed in Los Angeles. That performance has long been heralded as one of the greatest performance of its kind in history. The first part of the piece is moderately soft, and gradually builds to the climax when he sings out "Vincero!". The element of softness is defined as intensity, which falls under timbre. How high or how soft a musical note is played or sung is defined as intensity. Pavarotti also had a distinct tone when he sung that song. Everyone's voice has a distinct tone, which sets us apart.

In this tutorial, we will discuss all these important aspects of music, and how they come together when one composes music. Let's go into greater detail about these basics, and I'll explain how exactly they lay the foundation for composing music.

© **Copyright 2014 by dreamfish LLC - All rights reserved.**

This document is geared towards providing reliable information in regards to the topic and issue covered. The publication is sold with the idea that the publisher is not required to render accounting, officially permitted, or otherwise, qualified services. If advice is necessary, legal or professional, a practiced individual in the profession should be ordered.

- From a Declaration of Principles which was accepted and approved equally by a Committee of the American Bar Association and a Committee of Publishers and Associations.

In no way is it legal to reproduce, duplicate, or transmit any part of this document in either electronic means or in printed format. Recording of this publication is strictly prohibited and any storage of this document is not allowed unless with written permission from the publisher. All rights reserved.

The information provided herein is stated to be truthful and consistent, in that any liability, in terms of inattention or otherwise, by any usage or abuse of any policies, processes, or directions contained within is solely and completely the responsibility of the recipient reader. Under no circumstances will any legal responsibility or blame be held against the publisher for any reparation, damages, or monetary loss due to the information herein, either directly or indirectly.

Respective authors own all copyrights not held by the publisher.

The information herein is offered for informational purposes solely, and is universal as so. The presentation of the information is without contract or any type of guarantee assurance.

The trademarks that are used are without any consent, and the publication of the trademark is without permission or backing by the trademark owner. All trademarks and brands within this book are for clarifying purposes only and are the owned by the owners themselves, not affiliated with this document.

CHAPTER 1 – REVIEWING THE BASICS

We discussed the basic elements of music as being melody, harmony, rhythm, form and timbre. In this chapter we'll discuss everything possible about the basics of music, for those who are unfamiliar and for those who need refreshing. Don't skip this part, however, no matter how versed you think you are in these subjects. It is the longest chapter because this is where the foundations are laid for composing music.

Melody

Melody is the most important aspect of Western Music, especially popular music. It is the melody that will evoke the most memories when listening to a song or musical piece. This is so because of the way we process music. When we think of the song we heard on the radio an hour ago, notice that the beat and the harmony is forced into the background. It is the melody and the lyrics, if there are lyrics, that are forefront. This is because we break music down when we listen to it subconsciously, and the element of music that we will most likely be remembering is the melody. Johann Kirnberger, a renowned theorist in the 18th century, said this about melody:

"The true goal of music—its proper enterprise—is melody. All the parts of harmony have as their ultimate purpose only beautiful melody. Therefore the question of which is the more significant, melody or harmony, is futile. Beyond doubt, the means is subordinate to the end."

The man couldn't have spoken truer words. While harmony brings out the richness of the music, all else points to the melody. Different genres of music interpret and manipulate melody in different ways. In jazz, for example, the melody is usually termed as the "lead" or the "head", which introduces the idea of the song and then is improvised and built upon. With pop music, basically all music that is popular in today's world, the songs usually have one or two melodies that are done in the verses and/or chorus. They may vary from time to time, but they pretty much use the same system.

In later chapters we will discuss classical music and how music has evolved over the years; how these composers manipulated elements such as melody. But to gloss over it a bit, the melody of the piece was usually brought in at the beginning, which is termed a "theme", and then variations of that theme were introduced throughout the piece. Take Bach's Brandenburg Concerto for instance: all the strings play the melody then branch off into different variations.

Harmony

Without harmony, most Western music would sound like Eastern music or the Gregorian chants of old. Harmony makes the music sound richer, and provides a much richer experience when listening to a piece of music. Harmony should always point to the melody, not take away from it. When harmony takes away from the melody, usually confusion and chaos take place, and this perplexes the listener. To refresh, harmony is a group of notes being played simultaneously. These groups are called chords. Now, when chords are played along with the melody line, a chord progression takes place. Let's take for example, Barbershop Quartets. These groups dazzle audiences with extremely tight four-part harmonies. With every word, there is a different chord used. Why is a different chord used? Why not just use the same chord over and over again. Well, the same chord could be used over and over again, but it would clash with the melody and cause confusion at times. This is why it's important for composers to know what key signatures are.

Keys and Musical Scales

The key is basically the tonic note or chord in which the piece is derived from. Tonic, in this sense, means "root". In this tutorial, we'll focus on the two main types of keys: majors and minors. When we play the scale, like "do-re-mi", the tonic note of that scale would be the first one, or in this case, "do".

"Do-re-mi" is an example of a major scale, based on its form. We won't go into much detail, but the major scale goes by this formula: root-tone-tone-semitone-tone-tone-tone-semitone, where the tone means one whole step and a semitone is defined as a half-step. On a piano, there are white and black keys. If you play any white key, most likely (not all the time) the absolute nearest key will be a black key. If you play from that white key to the black key, it's a half-step, or semitone. If you play to another white key and there's a black key between those keys, it's a tone. There are times when you'll play from a white key to another white key and it's a semitone, while sometimes you'll play from a white key to a black key and it's a tone. It's for you to study the keyboard and know the differences.

Now that we established that, we can now discuss scales in further detail. When we play a major scale, we play by the formula above. So if we start at C, the tone above that will be D, then the tone above that will be E, and so forth. This scale is called C major. Music is written in different majors and minors, and whichever song has the tonic on C (whether it starts on C or ends on C in the major scale), is C Major - the key. You can write music in whatever key you wish. Whether it be C, Db, F#, whatever you choose. Songs in the major key usually sound happy and joyous. Minors, however, are dark and mysterious and sometimes sad. Minor scales follow a different formula than majors. There are different types of minors, but the most basic type follows this pattern: root-tone-semitone-tone-tone-semitone-tone#-semitone. Now you might be wondering what tone# means. This means you go a tone, then go an extra semitone.

When you understand majors and minors, and chord progressions that you can use in these keys, you understand enough to write your own songs. We'll discuss this later on.

Form and Timbre

Form is a term used to describe how a musical piece is structured. If you are writing a pop song, then you might very well structure the song like this: verse-chorus-verse-chorus-bridge-chorus. Musical form varies among the genres and among cultures. The composer can use any musical form he wishes.

Timbre is a very important aspect when writing music. You have to know how you want your song to be delivered because if it doesn't have the right direction, it will give the wrong message. Just think of "Silent Night" played by a heavy metal rock band blaring the song over the speakers. Does that make sense? No it doesn't. If you're writing a song about a breakup, then you know you will want your song to have a somber mood. You will make sure the singer's voice, whether yours or somebody else's, gives off the sense that something went wrong and he or she is not happy. The music here will be soft to moderately loud, but not any above that. The song will most likely be in a minor key. In the third chapter, Conceptualization, we'll use everything we learned here to make our own breakup song.

Chord Progressions

Finally, let's talk about one of the most important aspects of songwriting: making chord progressions. Once you know your majors and minors, chord progressions will come naturally. In a musical scale, there are usually eight notes played. In ancient times and in other parts of the world, you could have 6, 7 or even 12, but I digress. We usually denote these as Roman Numerals, so the first note in the C Major Scale, which is C, would take on I; the second note, which is D, would take on II; the third note, which is E, would take on III, and so on. So the last note, which is C again, will have VIII. Usually, to get rid of redundancy, we note that last note as I again. The most popular chord progression in Western Music is I-IV-V-I. Now let's look at that from the perspective of the key of C Major.

I in this case is denoting C, and since it's a chord, it will be the C Major chord - the tonic. The next chord to come is IV. If we count our scale, we'll find IV to be F. So, here, based on the key being played, it will be F Major. Next up is V, and you guessed it, G Major. If you play it on the guitar and cycle it over and over again, you will hear the melodies of a lot of songs in your head in an instant. You might even hear an original melody, which in that case, you should get a pen and paper.

There are so many other chord progressions used. Another popular one is I-II-V-I. Another is I-III-VI-V. In those two examples, the II and VI in the C major scale would both be minors. Why? If they were majors, they would deviate from the C major scale. Take for instance, II. If we formed a triad (chord of three notes usually spaced out I-III-VI in its original form) in the major, we would have D-F#-A. There is no F# in C Major, hence II could only mean D-F-A, which is D minor. Of course, there are exceptions to the rule, and the major second is a wonderful addition at times to lead to the V. VI is A minor, and it is C Major's relative minor. The VI is always the relative minor of the major. Relative minors add substance to your song, and the use of it is highly encouraged. These chord progressions are often used in the minor keys as well.

CHAPTER 2 – THE CONCEPTUALIZATION PHASE

So now that we've understood all of the basics, let's see how we can compose our music. The most important aspect of the process is the idea stage. Musicians often get their inspiration for songs from different life events, world events, nature, taking a bath, browsing the internet, etc. What we're saying is, once you're alive, you will be inspired to pen something down into a song. Sometimes, however, musicians meet upon a "writer's block" of their own when they have to compose a song as their job. These musicians have often have to go out seeking inspiration to meet deadlines. There are times even when you're writing a song for the fun of it, and you are in the middle and don't know what to do next. Here we'll outline different ways in which the writer's block can be overcome and you can get down to writing an awesome piece.

Music composition begins in the mind, and having a clear mind and an acceptance of who you are is important for the creativity juices to flow. The first step is to go into the composition stage with the mind of a child; go writing something simple, yet fun and understandable. Don't go in there thinking of writing something like what only Bach or Beethoven could conjure up. Go into composition without the mindset of being great, which will result in you coming up with nice melodies and harmonies.

It is important to also listen to other people's music. If you want to compose an instrumental piece, say for the piano, listen to the works of Chopin, Beethoven and Rachmaninov first. Listen to how they structure their music. If you want your music to sound more modern, listen to how modern day musicians structure their music. The more you listen to other people's music, the more your horizons will widen. Go further than Katy Perry and Nicki Minaj. Listen to them yes, but an artist shouldn't take up more than 5% of your listening time. Listen to different genres, even the ones you don't like. Listen to how different melodies and harmonies are used, then you will be able to think of your very own ways of doing things.

Go outside, do the things you love. Inspiration comes in a variety of ways and places. When you are doing the things that you like, think of the melodies that you came up with while taking a shower and repeat it over and over in your head. When you do this, you will be able to expand on what you already have and move away from the writer's block. After the inspiration, comes the practice. It's time to move towards your musical instrument and start writing.

With the sufficient knowledge of music theory in hand, sit around the piano and think of a melody and think of a way to accompany your melody with different harmonies and rhythms. We'll use an example to help in this process. For this exercise, we'll arrange "Mary Had A Little Lamb" in the minor key and make it sound like a breakup song, which we said we will do in the previous chapter.

These are the lyrics that we'll use:

> *Mary had a little lamb*
>
> *Little lamb, little lamb.*
>
> *Mary had a little lamb*
>
> *So why'd he have to go.*

Silly I know, but I'll admit I'm not very good with breakup song lyrics. Let's just pretend lamb is a euphemism for boyfriend. So, we have the idea. Now we have the melody in our head. Of course, we are composing, not arranging. "Mary Had A Little Lamb" does not exist in this Universe. You need to come up with a melody. Let's use the original melody, with a twist. For it to be a breakup song, it has to be in the minor key, since we're sad about the breakup. So, in C minor, the first line of the song will be: Eb-D-C-D-Eb-Eb-Eb. The second line will be: D-D-D-D-G-G. The third line will repeat the first and the last line will be Eb-D-C-D-Eb-D-C. When played at a Grave pace, it sounds really sad. Now we need the harmony since we have the melody. With the knowledge gleaned from our discussions about the basics of music theory and from other sources, you can bang out chords you can play along with the melody. Do not be elaborate. A simple chord progression would use I, IV and V chords only. Make sure whatever chord you use matches the melody used.

The conceptualizing stage is a fun stage. Making your own music from one single melody is fun and rewarding, and you'll feel like Mozart when you do this. However, you will NEVER become a master at this craft if you don't become an addict to composition. You have to keep writing pieces, no matter how simple they are. Once you get the hang of it, you will be writing more elaborate pieces, and who knows, you could be composing the score for a movie one day. It's important to dream, put in the hours, and stick to the plan.

CHAPTER 3 – COMPUTER SOFTWARE FOR COMPOSERS

Many composers use different software to compose their music. The two most popular ones are Finale and Sibelius. These composition tools allow you to write your own sheet music, and even help with the writing process. Some use audio production tools for composition, and we'll discuss that in the next chapter. Finale is used by many professionals but Sibelius is a favorite among beginners and music students because of its friendly GUI (graphical user interface). We'll discuss using Sibelius to write a score for your song. You can get Sibelius from Avid's website and you can try it for free.

Sibelius is an excellent software program for beginners as mentioned before. To use composition tools, it is very important that you are versed in music theory, because if you aren't, it doesn't make sense. Using this tutorial alone won't help, as only the surface was touched. There are many resources online that you can use, especially on Youtube.

When scoring a song, these three most important things must be known first: clef, time signature and key signature. The Clef is the sign at the beginning of your music that tells you what the notes on the lines and the spaces are. Without the clef those lines and spaces would just be lines and spaces. There are two basic clef types: the treble clef, and the bass clef. The first line (bottom line) on the treble clef is E, while the first line on the bass clef is G. See why the clef is so important? The treble clef looks like a big 'S' while the bass clef looks like a big comma with two dots beside it. Most often, what you play from your right hand is the treble clef while what you play from your left hand is the bass clef. This is not always the case, but it mostly is. The melody for the song we wrote in the previous chapter will most likely go in the treble staff, while the accompaniment will go in the bass. Next up in important things to know is the key signature. These signatures follow the clef and are denoted by a group of sharps, flats or nothing at all. When it's nothing there, then the key is C Major or A Minor. For our Mary song, it's C Minor, hence it would have three flats (please do more reading on majors and their relative minors to fully understand. E Major also has three flats). Next up is the time signature, which basically tells you how many beats are in each bar. For this song, the time signature is 4/4.

The software allows you to put these three things first before you do any note-inputting. After you have established your clef, time signature and key signatures, you're ready to input your notes. It is important to know the values of each note. For this song, you will be using merely crotchets. Crotchets have a value of one beat. After you are done note-inputting, the dynamics, or the intensity of the piece must be put in at strategic places. If you look on a score, you will often see a boldened 'f', 'mf', or 'p', etc. These denote how loudly or softly you must sing or play the note or group of notes. 'f' stands for 'forte' and means loud. 'p' stands for 'piano' and means soft. 'm' stands for 'moderately' and when used before a 'p' or 'f' makes the note played a little more or less than it is.

Use the "Input" menu, find Text, and place your Tempo. For this piece, you will want Grave as your tempo. The Italian for Grave (music directions are written in Italian) is Lento.

After this, place your Title, the Composer name, and you have just written your very first score!

(For more information on Sibelius, go to their site to view their documentation.)

CHAPTER 4 – AUDIO PRODUCTION

Digital audio workstations, or DAWs for short, are electronic systems and software designed solely for recording and audio production. For the average musician, he will have a keyboard/guitar, microphone and a computer. Professional audio engineers have more advanced DAWs with modules, control boards, speakers, etc. Many composers and songwriters opt to work with these professionals, often called producers, instead of making professional tracks themselves. The art of good audio production takes years of practice and effort, just like composition and composing with software like Sibelius. Software DAWs try to bring the beauty of hardware DAWs into your computer, no matter how powerful it may be. These Sofware DAWs are also called Music Sequencers. Some examples include Ableton, Adobe Audition, Audacity, FL Studio, Garageband, Logic Pro, Reason, etc. These work by having working with tracks. Each track has a section of the music in it, and tracks can be laid on top of each other so that they can be played simultaneously. This makes it possible for one man to produce and orchestral effect, as he could have one track have the violin sounds, another one having the percussion sounds and another having the brass sounds. When played together it becomes awe-inspiring music, but when each track is played by itself, it sounds monotonous.

Music Sequencers can have software instruments as well, such as the piano or guitar, so that the use of the actual instruments wouldn't be necessary. This is why a lot of musicians tend to skip the music notation phase and go straight to the production. If you want to digitally produce the music you've just written, what you could do is to export the song as a MIDI file, and import it into your DAW of choice. Each instrument in the Midi file will show up as one track, depending on your configurations. You can use this to even produce and orchestral sound just from your piano score.

CONCLUSION

Thank you for purchasing this book! I hope it helped you better envision yourself as a Composer. Composing music is a feasible goal for anyone who wants to do it, given that it takes the following three things:

1. a general understanding of the basics discussed in this book,
2. a passion and love for music,
3. a commitment of time to just keep-on-keeping-on, composing songs over and over again.

Start by creating some easy tunes at first before putting any pressure on yourself to be the next musical genius. That way, you'll get the hang of it and I promise it gets easier and easier for each song you compose. Most importantly though: Have fun with it! Music is supposed to be a release of emotions and creativity – one of life's great pleasures. Enjoy it!

Thank you for purchasing this book, and good luck! Oh also, if you found this book helpful, please take the time to share your thoughts and post a review on Amazon. It'd be greatly appreciated!

Printed in Great Britain
by Amazon